D1623939

little book of

Tequila
Cocktails

little book of

Tequila
Cocktails

Wayne Collins

hamlyn

An Hachette Livre UK Company
First published in 2000 by Hamlyn, a division of Octopus Publishing Group Limited,
2–4 Heron Quays, London E14 4JP
Copyright © 2000 Octopus Publishing Group Ltd

Distributed in the United States and Canada by Sterling Publishing Co., Inc.
387 Park Avenue South, New York, NY 10016-8810

British Library Cataloguing-in-Publication Data
A catalogue record for this book is available from the British Library

ISBN-13: 978-0-600-61771-6
ISBN-10: 0-600-61771-8

Printed in China

10 9 8 7 6 5 4 3 2 1

Notes for American readers

The measure that has been used in the recipes is based on
a bar jigger, which is 45 ml (1½ fl oz). If preferred, a different
volume can be used providing the proportions are kept
constant within a drink and suitable adjustments are made
to spoon measurements, where they occur.

Standard level spoon measurements are used in all recipes.
1 tablespoon = one 15 ml spoon
1 teaspoon = one 5 ml spoon
Imperial and metric measurements have been given in
some of the recipes. Use one set of measurements only and
not a mixture of both.

UK	US
caster sugar	granulated sugar
cocktail cherries	maraschino cherries
cocktail stick	toothpick
double cream	heavy cream
drinking chocolate	presweetened cocoa powder
icing sugar	confectioners' sugar
jug	pitcher
lemon rind	lemon peel or zest
single cream	light cream
soda water	club soda

Contents

STRICTLY MARGARITAS 8
The Margarita is the most famous of all tequila cocktails and, because it is such a great drink, it has inspired a host of variations.

COOL CLASSICS 26
These delectable mixes show you just what glorious cocktails can be based on tequila.

LONG SHOTS 52
In these chapter, fruit juices of all sorts and fruit liqueurs blend deliciously with tequila and ice to make a series of long refreshing drinks.

CREAMY & EXOTIC COCKTAILS 82
The exotic flavours and generous servings of fresh cream in this chapter add a rich smoothness to tequila cocktails. You need to be on your guard with these drinks as the cream disguises the strength of the alcohol.

Introduction

Tequila has a bizarre and exotic quality that is missing from the other major spirits. Distilled from the root of the maguey or blue agave, a cactus-like plant which actually belongs to the amaryllis family, it is Mexico's contribution to the great drinks of the world.

Pulque was the first drink to be produced from the agave. It is made by fermenting the sap from the plant, and dates back to prehispanic times. A low alcohol drink, it is still drunk today. When the Spaniards conquered Mexico in 1519–21, one of the many things they introduced was the art of distilling and they turned their attention to pulque. During the late 18th and early 19th century it was realized that the best *aguardiente de agave*, as the distilled spirit was known, was produced around the town of Tequila in the state of Jalisco.

By the late 19th century the commercial cultivation of agaves in Mexico had begun and by the 1870s there were about a dozen distilleries. The United States was the first, and is still the most important export market for tequila, but it was not until the mid-sixties that tequila burst upon the rest of the world. By the seventies the demand had led to a need for regulations to define tequila and to protect the name, limiting its production to tequila produced in the state of Jalisco.

Tequila has been described as having a smooth sharpness. There are several types. Tequila blanco, the original version, is colourless while tequila reposado (gold) is aged in oak barrels for up to 11 months. Tequila añejo has longer ageing. Mezcal is an another agave-distilled spirit but with a different style from tequila.

Mezcals labelled '*con gusano*' contain a worm. Despite widespread belief, tequila does not contain a worm.

The traditional way to drink tequila is with a pinch of salt. The practice is to lick the salt from between the thumb and forefinger, then knock back the tequila from a shot glass and suck a wedge of lime or lemon. As a variation, sips from a glass of tequila may be alternated with sips of sangrita, a highly spiced tomato juice. Salt is also used for rimming the glass of the Margarita, a delicious concoction of tequila, Cointreau and fresh lime juice and the most famous tequila cocktail of all. It originated in the late thirties at the hotel bar in the Rancho la Gloria, Rosarita Beach, Tijuana, where it was thought to be created by Danny Herrera for the actress Marjorie King, who was allergic to all spirits except tequila. He named it Margarita – the Spanish for Marjorie.

Bar Equipment
Cocktails are all the better for being made correctly. A well-stocked home bar should contain the following equipment: a cocktail shaker for drinks which are shaken, a mixing glass (also called a bar glass) and a long-handled bar spoon for drinks that are stirred rather than shaken, and a blender for making drinks with ingredients such as fresh fruit and egg white. A set of bar measures; a canelle knife for removing spirals of lime, lemon and orange rind; a lemon squeezer; ice containers and tongs for lifting ice cubes; and a salt saucer for rimming glasses are all important for tequila cocktails, as are a chopping board and a sharp knife.

Sugar Syrup
Using sugar syrup is the most practical way of sweetening a drink. Since the sugar is already dissolved it does not need lengthy stirring to blend it into a cold drink. Pour equal quantities of sugar and water (6 tablespoons of each is a practical amount) into a small saucepan and bring to the boil, stirring to dissolve the sugar, then boil for 1–2 minutes without stirring. Sugar syrup can be stored in the refrigerator in a sterilized bottle for up to 2 months.

Strictly Margaritas

Original
Margarita

3 lime wedges
fine sea salt
1¼ measures tequila
¾ measure Cointreau
1¼ measures fresh
    lime juice
4–5 ice cubes
lime wheel, to decorate

Dampen the rim of a chilled cocktail glass with 1 of the lime wedges then dip the rim into fine sea salt. Pour the tequila, Cointreau and lime juice into a cocktail shaker. Squeeze the juice from the remaining 2 lime wedges into the shaker, squeeze the wedges to release the oils in the skin then drop the wedges into the shaker. Add the ice cubes and shake vigorously for about 10 seconds. Strain the cocktail into the chilled glass and decorate with a lime wheel.

Serves 1

Floreciente

1 orange slice
fine sea salt
crushed ice
1¼ measures tequila gold
¾ measure Cointreau
¾ measure fresh
    lemon juice
¾ measure fresh blood
    orange juice
blood orange wedge, to
    decorate

Dampen the rim of a 300 ml (½ pint) old-fashioned glass with an orange slice then dip the glass into fine sea salt and fill it with crushed ice. Pour the tequila, Cointreau, lemon juice and blood orange juice into a cocktail shaker, shake vigorously for 10 seconds then strain into the old-fashioned glass. Decorate with a blood orange wedge.

Serves 1

Cadillac

3 lime wedges
fine sea salt
4–5 ice cubes
1¼ measures tequila gold
½ measure Cointreau
1¼ measures fresh
    lime juice
2 teaspoons Grand
    Marnier
lime slice, to decorate

Dampen the rim of a chilled cocktail glass with 1 of the lime wedges, then dip the rim into fine sea salt. Pour the tequila, Cointreau and lime juice into a cocktail shaker. Squeeze the juice from the 2 remaining lime wedges into the shaker, pressing the rind to release its oils. Drop the wedges into the shaker. Add the ice cubes and shake vigorously for 10 seconds then strain the drink into the glass. Drizzle the Grand Marnier over the top of the drink. Decorate with a lime slice.

Serves 1

Pink Cadillac Convertible

3 lime wedges
fine sea salt
ice cubes
1¼ measures tequila gold
½ measure Cointreau
¾ measure fresh
   lime juice
¾ measure cranberry
   juice
lime wedge, to decorate
¾ measure Grand
   Marnier

Dampen the rim of a 300 ml (½ pint) old-fashioned glass with 1 of the lime wedges, then dip the rim into fine sea salt and fill the glass with ice cubes. Pour the tequila, Cointreau, lime juice and cranberry juice into a cocktail shaker. Squeeze the juice from the 2 remaining lime wedges into the shaker, pressing the rind to release its oils. Drop the wedges into the shaker. Add 4–5 ice cubes and shake vigorously for 10 seconds then strain the drink into the glass. Decorate with a lime wedge. Pour the Grand Marnier into a shot glass and serve it on the side. This should be poured on to the top of the cocktail just before drinking.

Serves 1

Cobalt Margarita

1 lime wedge
fine sea salt
1¼ measures tequila
2 teaspoons Cointreau
½ measure blue Curaçao
¾ measure fresh
   lime juice
¾ measure fresh
   grapefruit juice
4–5 ice cubes
lime rind spiral, to
   decorate

Dampen the rim of a chilled
cocktail glass with a lime wedge
then dip it into fine sea salt.
Pour the tequila, Cointreau,
blue Curaçao, lime juice and
grapefruit juice into a cocktail
shaker. Add the ice cubes and
shake vigorously for 10 seconds
then strain into the cocktail glass.
Decorate with a lime rind spiral.

Serves 1

Tip

To make a citrus spiral,
pare the rind from the
fruit with a canelle knife
or vegetable peeler then
wind it tightly round a
glass swizzle stick.

Playa del Mar

1 orange slice
light brown sugar and
    sea salt mixture
ice cubes
1¼ measures tequila gold
¾ measure Grand
    Marnier
2 teaspoons fresh
    lime juice
¾ measure cranberry
    juice
¾ measure fresh
    pineapple juice

to decorate
pineapple wedge
orange rind spiral

Dampen the rim of a sling glass with the orange slice then dip it into the brown sugar and sea salt mixture. Fill the glass with ice cubes. Pour the tequila, Grand Marnier, lime juice, cranberry juice and pineapple juice into a cocktail shaker. Fill the shaker with ice cubes and shake vigorously for 10 seconds then strain into the sling glass. Decorate with a pineapple wedge and an orange rind spiral.

Serves 1

Ruby Rita

1¼ measures fresh pink
    grapefruit juice
fine sea salt
ice cubes
1¼ measures tequila gold
¾ measure Cointreau
pink grapefruit wedge, to
    decorate

Dampen the rim of 300 ml (½ pint) old-fashioned glass with some pink grapefruit juice and dip it into fine sea salt. Fill the glass with ice cubes. Pour the tequila, Cointreau and pink grapefruit juice into a cocktail shaker, fill with more ice and shake vigorously. Strain into the old-fashioned glass and decorate with a pink grapefruit wedge.

Serves 1

Forest Fruit

1 lime wedge
brown sugar
2 blackberries
2 raspberries
2 teaspoons Chambord
2 teaspoons Crème
   de Mure
1¼ measures tequila
2 teaspoons Cointreau
1¼ measures fresh
   lemon juice
crushed ice

to decorate
lemon slices
blackberry
raspberry

Chambord is a black raspberry liqueur and Crème de Mure is a blackberry one.

Dampen the rim of an old-fashioned glass with a lime wedge and dip it into brown sugar. Drop the blackberries and raspberries into the glass and muddle to a pulp with the back of a spoon or a porcelain pestle. Stir in the Chambord and Crème de Mure. Pour in the tequila, Cointreau and lemon juice, fill with crushed ice and stir gently, lifting the muddled berries from the bottom of the glass. Decorate with lemon slices, a blackberry and a raspberry.

Serves 1

Maracuja

1 fresh ripe passion fruit
1¼ measures tequila gold
1 tablespoon Creole
    Shrub
¾ measure fresh
    lime juice
2 teaspoons Cointreau
1 teaspoon passion
    fruit syrup
4–5 ice cubes
physalis (Cape
    gooseberry), to
    decorate

Creole Shrub is a golden-coloured rum, flavoured with orange peel.

Cut the passion fruit in half and scoop the flesh into a cocktail shaker. Add the tequila, Creole Shrub, lime juice, Cointreau, passion fruit syrup and ice cubes and shake vigorously for 10 seconds. Strain through a small fine sieve into a chilled cocktail glass. Decorate with a physalis.

Serves 1

Tip

It is important to use a really ripe passion fruit for this drink.

Cool Classics

South of the Border

Alleluia

Mezcarita

Tequini

Sour Apple

Chapala

Ananas e Coco

Honey Water

Bloody Maria

Frozen Strawberry

Japanese Slipper

Mockingbird

Pancho Villa

Coco Loco

Tequila Sunset

South of the Border

1¼ measures tequila
¾ measure Kahlúa
1¼ measures fresh
    lime juice
4–5 ice cubes

to decorate
lime wedge
brown sugar
ground coffee

Kahlúa is as Mexican as tequila. It is a liqueur made from Mexican coffee beans.

Pour the tequila, Kahlúa and lime juice into a cocktail shaker. Add the ice cubes and shake vigorously for 10 seconds then strain into a chilled cocktail glass. To decorate, take a lime wedge, press one side into a saucer of sugar and the other side into a saucer of ground coffee, and serve on the side.

Serves 1

Alleluia

¾ measure tequila
½ measure blue Curaçao
2 teaspoons
   maraschino syrup
dash of egg white
¾ measure fresh
   lemon juice
ice cubes
100 ml (3½ fl oz)
   bitter lemon

to decorate
lemon slice
maraschino cherry
mint sprig

Pour the tequila, blue Curaçao, maraschino syrup, egg white and lemon juice into a cocktail shaker, add 4–5 ice cubes and shake vigorously. Fill a 350 ml (12 fl oz) highball glass with ice cubes and strain the drink over the ice. Top up with the bitter lemon and stir gently. Decorate with a lemon slice, cherry and mint sprig.

Serves 1

Tip
For maraschino syrup, use the syrup from the jar of maraschino cherries.

Mezcarita

1 lemon wedge
chilli salt
1¼ measures mezcal
¾ measure Cointreau
1¼ measures fresh
    lemon juice
4–5 ice cubes
lemon rind spiral, to
    decorate

Dampen the rim of a chilled cocktail glass with the wedge of lemon and dip it into chilli salt. Pour the mezcal, Cointreau and lemon juice into a cocktail shaker, add the ice cubes and shake vigorously. Strain into the cocktail glass and decorate with the lemon rind spiral.

Serves 1

cool classics

Tequini

ice cubes

3 dashes orange bitters

75 ml (3 fl oz) tequila
 blanco

2 teaspoons dry French
 vermouth, preferably
 Noilly Prat

black olive, to decorate

This is the Mexican equivalent of a martini, with tequila replacing the gin and the orange bitters adding an exotic tang. It is one of the few drinks decorated with a black olive rather than a green one.

Fill a mixing glass with ice cubes then add the orange bitters and tequila. Stir gently with a bar spoon for 10 seconds. Take a chilled cocktail glass and add the vermouth, film the inside of the glass with the vermouth then tip it out. Stir the bitters and tequila for a further 10 seconds and strain into the chilled glass. Decorate with a large black olive.

Serves 1

Sour Apple

1¼ measures tequila

2 teaspoons Cointreau

1 tablespoon apple
    schnapps

¾ measure fresh
    lime juice

¾ measure dry
    apple juice

4–5 ice cubes

wedge of Granny Smith
    apple, to decorate

Pour the tequila, Cointreau,
apple schnapps, lime juice and
apple juice into a cocktail shaker,
add the ice cubes and shake
vigorously for 10 seconds then
strain into a chilled cocktail glass.
Decorate with a Granny Smith
apple wedge.

Serves 1

Chapala

1¼ measures tequila
¾ measure Cointreau
¾ measure fresh
    lemon juice
¾ measure fresh
    orange juice
2 teaspoons grenadine
orange rind spiral, to
    decorate

Pour the tequila, Cointreau, lemon juice and orange juice into a cocktail shaker. Add the grenadine and shake vigorously for 10 seconds then strain into a chilled cocktail glass. Decorate with an orange rind spiral.

Serves 1

Ananas & Coco

1¼ measures tequila gold
¾ measure coconut syrup
1 large chunk fresh
    pineapple
1¼ measures pineapple
    juice
crushed ice
pineapple wedge, to
    decorate

Put the tequila, coconut syrup, pineapple chunk and pineapple juice into a blender. Add a handful of crushed ice, blend for 20 seconds then pour into a wine goblet. Decorate with a pineapple wedge.

Serves 1

Honey Water

4–5 ice cubes
1¼ measures tequila gold
¾ measure sweet
    vermouth
3 dashes Angostura
    bitters
3 dashes Peychaud
    bitters
2 teaspoons Grand
    Marnier

to decorate
maraschino cherry
orange rind spiral

Put the ice cubes into a mixing glass, pour in the tequila, vermouth and both bitters and stir gently for 10 seconds. Put the Grand Marnier into a chilled cocktail glass, film the inside of the glass with the Grand Marnier then tip it out. Stir the contents of the mixing glass again for 10 seconds then strain into the cocktail glass. Decorate with a maraschino cherry and an orange rind spiral.

Serves 1

Bloody Maria

1 lime wedge

celery salt

black pepper

ice cubes

1¼ measures tequila

2 teaspoons medium
   sherry

2 dashes Tabasco sauce

4 dashes Worcestershire
   sauce

1 tablespoon fresh
   lime juice

100 ml (3½ fl oz) fresh
   tomato juice

cayenne pepper

4–5 ice cubes

to decorate

celery stick

lime wedge

basil sprig

Dampen the rim of a 350 ml
(12 fl oz) old-fashioned glass with
a lime wedge then dip it into
celery salt and black pepper. Fill
a cocktail shaker with ice cubes
then add the tequila, sherry,
Tabasco sauce, Worcestershire
sauce, lime juice, tomato juice
and a pinch each of celery salt,
black pepper and cayenne
pepper. Add the ice cubes and
shake vigorously then pour into
the old-fashioned glass. Decorate
with the celery stick, lime wedge
and a basil sprig.

Serves 1

Frozen Strawberry

sugar
a small handful of
    crushed ice
2 measures tequila
1 measure strawberry
    liqueur
1 measure fresh
    lime juice
4 ripe strawberries
1 teaspoon Sugar Syrup
    (see page 7)
fresh strawberry,
    unhulled, to decorate

Dampen the rim of a chilled cocktail glass and dip it into the sugar. Put the crushed ice into a blender and pour in the tequila, strawberry liqueur and lime juice. Drop in the strawberries, add the sugar syrup and blend for a few seconds. Pour without straining into a cocktail glass and decorate with a strawberry.

Serves 1

Japanese Slipper

1 lime wedge
brown sugar
1¼ measures tequila
¾ measure Midori
1¼ measures fresh
    lime juice
4–5 ice cubes
lime wedge, to decorate

Midori is a Japanese melon liqueur. Combined with tequila and lime juice, it makes a delectable drink.

Dampen the rim of a chilled cocktail glass with a lime wedge then dip the rim into brown sugar. Pour the tequila, Midori and lime juice into a cocktail shaker and add the ice cubes. Shake vigorously for about 10 seconds then strain into the cocktail glass and decorate with a lime wedge.

Serves 1

Mockingbird

1¼ measures tequila
¾ measure green Crème
   de Menthe
1¼ measures fresh
   lime juice
4–5 ice cubes
lemon rind spiral, to
   decorate

Pour the tequila, crème de
menthe and lime juice into a
cocktail shaker. Add the ice
cubes, shake vigorously for about
10 seconds then strain into a
chilled cocktail glass. Decorate
with a lemon rind spiral.

Serves 1

Pancho Villa

1 measure tequila
½ measure Tia Maria
1 teaspoon Cointreau
4–5 ice cubes
brandied cherry, to
    decorate (optional)

Pour the tequila, Tia Maria and Cointreau into a cocktail shaker. Add the ice cubes, shake vigorously for about 10 seconds, then strain into a cocktail glass. Decorate with a brandied cherry, if liked.

Serves 1

Coco Loco

¾ measure white rum
¾ measure tequila
½ measure vodka
1 measure coconut
    cream
2 measures fresh
    lemon juice
3 ice cubes, cracked

to decorate
lemon rind twist
cocktail cherries

Pour the rum, tequila, vodka, coconut cream and lemon juice into a blender. Mix for 15 seconds. Put the ice cubes into a large goblet and pour over the drink. Decorate with the lemon rind twist and cherries and drink with a straw.

Serves 1

Tequila Sunset

1 measure tequila gold
1 measure fresh
    lemon juice
1 measure fresh
    orange juice
1 tablespoon honey
crushed ice
lemon rind spiral, to
    decorate

Put the tequila into a chilled cocktail glass, add the lemon juice and then the orange juice and stir. Drizzle the honey into the glass so that it falls in a layer to the bottom, add the crushed ice and decorate with a lemon rind spiral.

Serves 1

Long Shots

Texas Tea

Matador

Mexicola

Tijuana Sling

Rosarita Bay Breeze

El Diablo

Agave Julep

Sunburn

Gold Digger

Tequila Sunrise

Rooster Booster

Mexicana

Thai Sunrise

Pepper Eater

Baja Sour

Brooklyn Bomber

Tequila de Coco

Jalisco Swizzle

Acapulco

Desert Daisy

Long Island Iced Tea

Texas Tea

¾ measure tequila
1 tablespoon white rum
1 tablespoon Cointreau
2 teaspoons Sugar Syrup
(see page 7)
¾ measure fresh
lemon juice
¾ measure fresh
orange juice
100 ml (3½ fl oz) strong
fruit tea, chilled
ice cubes

to decorate
orange slice
lemon slice
mint sprig

Pour the tequila, rum, Cointreau, sugar syrup, lemon juice, orange juice and tea into a cocktail shaker, add a handful of ice cubes and shake vigorously. Fill a 350 ml (12 fl oz) sling glass with fresh ice cubes and strain the drink over them. Decorate with orange and lemon slices and a mint sprig.

Serves 1

Tip

One of the best teas to use as a base for this refreshing drink is a mixed berry tea. Its essential fruitiness blends very well with the citrus juices in Texas Tea.

Matador

1¼ measures tequila
¾ measure fresh
    lime juice
100 ml (3½ fl oz)
    pineapple juice
1 pineapple chunk
2 teaspoons Sugar Syrup
    (see page 7)
crushed ice

to decorate
pineapple wedge
lime rind spiral

Put the tequila, lime juice,
pineapple juice, pineapple chunk
and sugar syrup into a blender.
Add a handful of crushed ice and
blend for 15 seconds. Pour into a
highball glass and decorate with
a pineapple wedge and a lime
rind spiral.

Serves 1

Mexicola

4 lime wedges
crushed ice
1¼ measures tequila
150 ml (¼ pint) Coca-Cola

Put the lime wedges into a
350 ml (12 fl oz) highball glass
and crush gently with a pestle to
release the juices and oils. Fill the
glass with crushed ice, then pour
in the tequila and Coca-Cola. Stir
gently lifting the lime wedges
through the drink.

Serves 1

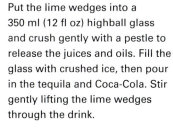

Tijuana Sling

1¼ measures tequila
¾ measure crème
    de cassis
¾ measure fresh
    lime juice
2 dashes Peychaud
    bitters
4–5 ice cubes
100 ml (3½ fl oz)
    ginger ale

to decorate
lime wheel
fresh blackcurrants or
    blueberries

Pour the tequila, crème de cassis, lime juice and Peychaud bitters into a cocktail shaker. Add the ice cubes and shake vigorously. Pour into a 350 ml (12 fl oz) sling glass then top up with ginger ale. Decorate with a lime wheel and fresh berries.

Serves 1

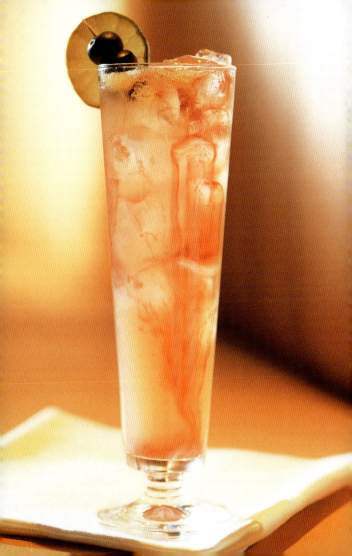

Rosarita Bay Breeze

ice cubes
1¼ measures tequila
150 ml (¼ pint) cranberry
    juice
1¼ measures pineapple
    juice
orange slice, to decorate

Put the ice cubes into a 350 ml (12 fl oz) highball glass and pour in the tequila and cranberry juice. Float the pineapple juice over the top of the drink and decorate with an orange slice.

Serves 1

El Diablo

ice cubes
1¼ measures tequila gold
¾ measure fresh
    lime juice
2 teaspoons grenadine
100 ml (3½ fl oz)
    ginger ale
lime slice, to decorate

Fill a 350 ml (12 fl oz) highball glass with ice cubes, then pour in the tequila, lime juice and grenadine. Top up with ginger ale and stir gently. Decorate with a lime slice.

Serves 1

Agave Julep

8 torn mint leaves

1 tablespoon Sugar
Syrup (see page 7)

1¼ measures tequila gold

1¼ measures fresh
lime juice

crushed ice

to decorate

lime wedge

mint sprig

Put the mint leaves into a 350 ml
(12 fl oz) highball glass and cover
with sugar syrup. Muddle with a
pestle to release the mint oils.
Add the tequila and lime juice, fill
the glass with crushed ice and
stir vigorously. Decorate with a
lime wedge and a mint sprig.

Serves 1

Sunburn

long shots

ice cubes
¾ measure tequila gold
1 tablespoon Cointreau
150 ml (¼ pint) cranberry
  juice
orange slice, to decorate

Fill a 350 ml (12 fl oz) highball glass with ice cubes, then pour in the tequila, Cointreau and cranberry juice. Decorate with an orange slice.

Serves 1

Tip
Decorative ice cubes make an unusual finishing touch for drinks. Half-fill an ice cube tray with water and freeze until firm. Prepare pieces of citrus rind or mint sprigs and dip into cold water. Add to the ice tray and freeze again. Top up with water and freeze until firm.

Gold Digger

ice cubes
¾ measure tequila gold
¾ measure golden rum
150 ml (¼ pint) fresh
    orange juice
2 teaspoons Grand
    Marnier
orange slice, to decorate

Put some ice cubes into a 350 ml
(12 fl oz) highball glass. Pour in
the tequila, rum and orange juice
and stir gently. Drizzle over the
Grand Marnier and decorate with
an orange slice.

Serves 1

Tequila Sunrise

5–6 ice cubes
1 measure tequila
100 ml (3½ fl oz) fresh
    orange juice
2 teaspoons grenadine

to decorate
star fruit slice
orange slice

The Tequila Sunrise is one of the cocktails which was popular during the Prohibition years in the United States, when the orange juice helped to disguise the unpleasant taste of raw alcohol.

Crack half the ice cubes and put them into a cocktail shaker. Add the tequila and orange juice and shake to mix. Put the remaining ice into a tall glass and strain the tequila into it. Slowly pour in the grenadine and allow it to settle. Just before serving, stir once. Decorate the glass with the star fruit and orange slice.

Serves 1

Rooster Booster

long shots

ice cubes
1¼ measures tequila
150 ml (¼ pint) fresh
    grapefruit juice
1 tablespoon grenadine
100 ml (3½ fl oz) soda
    water

to decorate
lime wheel
maraschino cherry

Put some ice cubes into a 350 ml
(12 fl oz) highball glass. Pour in
the tequila, grapefruit juice and
grenadine, stir gently then top up
with soda water. Decorate with a
lime wheel and a cherry.

Serves 1

Mexicana

8–10 ice cubes
1¼ measures tequila
¾ measure Framboise
¾ measure fresh
   lemon juice
100 ml (3½ fl oz)
   pineapple juice

to decorate
pineapple wedge
lemon slice

Framboise is an alcool blanc, a fruit liqueur (in this case a raspberry one) which is stored in glass rather than wood and so does not acquire any colour from the cask while it matures.

Put 4–5 ice cubes into a 350 ml (12 fl oz) highball glass. Pour the tequila, Framboise, lemon juice and pineapple juice into a cocktail shaker. Add 4–5 ice cubes and shake vigorously for about 10 seconds. Pour into the highball glass and decorate with a pineapple wedge and a lemon slice.

Serves 1

Thai Sunrise

½ ripe mango, peeled and
　　sliced
¾ measure tequila
1 tablespoon Cointreau
1 teaspoon grenadine
¾ measure fresh lime or
　　lemon juice
¾ measure Sugar Syrup
　　(see page 7)
2–3 ice cubes, cracked
lime slices, to decorate

Put all the ingredients into a
food processor and blend until
the ice is crushed. Pour into an
old-fashioned glass and decorate
with lime slices.

Serves 1

Pepper Eater

ice cubes
1¼ measures tequila
¾ measure Cointreau
100 ml (3½ fl oz)
    cranberry juice
1¼ measures fresh
    orange juice
orange slice, to decorate

Fill a 350 ml (12 fl oz) glass with ice cubes. Pour in the tequila, Cointreau, cranberry juice and orange juice and stir gently. Decorate with an orange slice.

Serves 1

Tip
Rolling an orange or any other citrus fruit hard on a board before you squeeze it helps extract more juice.

Baja Sour

1¼ measures tequila gold
2 teaspoons Sugar Syrup
(see page 7)
1¼ measures fresh
lemon juice
2 dashes orange bitters
½ egg white
4–5 ice cubes
1 tablespoon amontillado
sherry

to decorate
lemon slices
orange rind spiral

Pour the tequila, sugar syrup, lemon juice, orange bitters and egg white into a cocktail shaker. Add 4–5 ice cubes and shake vigorously. Pour into a 300 ml (½ pint) sour glass and drizzle over the sherry. Decorate with lemon slices and an orange rind spiral.

Serves 1

Brooklyn Bomber

5 ice cubes, crushed
1 measure tequila
½ measure Cointreau
½ measure cherry brandy
½ measure Galliano
1 measure lemon juice

to decorate
orange wheel
cocktail cherry

Put half the ice cubes into a cocktail shaker and add the tequila, Cointreau, cherry brandy, Galliano and lemon juice. Shake to mix. Put the remaining ice into a tall glass and pour over the drink. Decorate with the orange slice and cherry and serve with straws.

Serves 1

Tip

To make crushed ice, put some ice cubes into a strong polythene bag, seal it tightly, then hit it with a rolling pin to break up the ice.

Tequila de Coco

small handful of
    crushed ice
1 measure tequila
1 measure fresh
    lemon juice
1 measure coconut syrup
3 dashes maraschino
lemon slice, to decorate

Put the crushed ice into a blender and add the tequila, lemon juice, coconut syrup and maraschino. Blend for a few seconds then pour into a Collins glass and decorate with a lemon slice.

Serves 1

Jalisco Swizzle

crushed ice
3 dashes Angostura
   bitters
¾ measure tequila gold
¾ measure golden rum
1¼ measures fresh
   lime juice
¾ measure passion
   fruit juice
2 teaspoons Sugar Syrup
   (see page 7)
4–5 ice cubes
¾ measure soda water

Fill a chilled 350 ml (12 fl oz)
highball glass with crushed ice.
Put the Angostura into a cocktail
shaker, pour in the tequila, rum,
lime juice, passion fruit juice and
sugar syrup. Add the ice cubes
and shake vigorously then strain
into the highball glass. Top up
with soda and stir briefly until the
glass frosts. Decorate with a lime
wheel and a mint sprig.

Serves 1

to decorate
lime wheel
mint sprig

Acapulco

cracked ice
1 measure tequila
1 measure white rum
2 measures pineapple
   juice
1 measure fresh
   grapefruit juice
1 measure coconut syrup
ice cubes
pineapple wedge, to
   decorate

Put some cracked ice into a
cocktail shaker and pour in the
tequila, rum, pineapple juice,
grapefruit juice and coconut
syrup. Fill a tall glass with ice
cubes. Shake the drink and
pour it over the ice. Decorate
with a pineapple wedge and
serve with straws.

Serves 1

Tip
Fruit syrups can be
bought in good off-
licenses, department
stores or coffee shops.

Desert Daisy

crushed ice
1 measure tequila
1¼ measures fresh
    lime juice
2 teaspoons Sugar Syrup
    (see page 7)
1 tablespoon Fraise
    de Bois

to decorate
blackberry
strawberry
lime wedge
orange wedge
mint sprig

Half fill a 350 ml (12 fl oz) old-fashioned glass with crushed ice. Pour in the tequila, lime juice and sugar syrup and stir gently until the glass frosts. Add more crushed ice then float the Fraise de Bois on top. Decorate with a blackberry, a strawberry, a lime wedge, orange wedge and a mint sprig.

Serves 1

Long Island
Iced Tea

½ measure gin
½ measure vodka
½ measure white rum
½ measure tequila
½ measure Cointreau
¾ measure lemon juice
½ teaspoon Sugar Syrup
    (see page 7)
ice cubes
Coca-Cola

to decorate
lemon slices
mint sprigs

Long Island Iced Tea was popular during the Eighties. A highly intoxicating blend of colourless spirits and Coca-Cola, it really does look like iced tea.

Pour the gin, vodka, rum, tequila, Cointreau, lemon juice and sugar syrup into a mixing glass and stir thoroughly. Fill a tall glass almost full with ice cubes then strain the drink into it. Top up with Coca-Cola and decorate with lemon slices and mint sprigs.

Serves 1

Creamy & Exotic Cocktails

Silk Stocking

Brave Bull

Sombrero

Acapulco Bliss

Mexican Bulldog

Frostbite

Silk Stocking

drinking chocolate
  powder
¾ measure tequila
¾ measure white Crème
  de Cacao
100 ml (3½ fl oz) single
  cream
2 teaspoons grenadine
4–5 ice cubes

Dampen the rim of a chilled cocktail glass and dip it into the drinking chocolate powder. Pour the tequila, white Crème de Cacao, cream and grenadine into a cocktail shaker and add the ice cubes. Shake vigorously for 10 seconds then strain into the chilled cocktail glass.

Serves 1

Brave Bull

ice cubes
¾ measure tequila
¾ measure Kahlúa

Fill an old-fashioned glass with ice cubes, pour in the tequila and Kahlúa and stir gently.

Serves 1

Variations

BROWN COW

To turn a Brave Bull into a Brown Cow, add 1¼ measures single cream and stir to blend it in.

RAGING BULL

To turn a Brave Bull into a Raging Bull, add 1 teaspoon flaming Sambucca.

Sombrero

¾ measure tequila gold
¾ measure dark Crème
de Cacao
100 ml (3½ fl oz) single
cream
4–5 ice cubes
grated nutmeg, to
decorate

Pour the tequila, Crème de Cacao
and cream into a cocktail shaker.
Add the ice cubes and shake
vigorously for 10 seconds then
strain into a chilled cocktail glass.
To decorate, sprinkle the top of
the drink with grated nutmeg.

Serves 1

Tip
Crème de Cacao, the
chocolate liqueur, comes
in two versions, dark and
white. Choose according
to how you want your
drink to look. Combining
the dark version in a
Sombrero with tequila
gold and cream results in
a subtle coffee-coloured
drink.

Acapulco Bliss

¾ measure tequila
1 tablespoon Pisang
    Ambon (banana
    liqueur)
2 teaspoons Galliano
¾ measure fresh
    lemon juice
¾ measure single cream
100 ml (3½ fl oz) passion
    fruit juice
4–5 ice cubes

to decorate
lemon slices
pineapple wedge
mint sprig

Pour the tequila, Pisang Ambon, Galliano, lemon juice, cream and passion fruit juice into a cocktail shaker, add the ice cubes and shake vigorously. Pour into a 350 ml (12 fl oz) sling glass and decorate with lemon slices, a pineapple wedge and a mint sprig.

Serves 1

Mexican Bulldog

ice cubes
¾ measure tequila
¾ measure Kahlúa
1¼ measures single
    cream
100 ml (3½ fl oz)
    Coca-Cola
drinking chocolate
    powder, to decorate

Put some ice cubes into a 375 g (12 oz) highball glass. Pour in the tequila, Kahlúa and cream then top up with Coca-Cola. Stir gently and serve decorated with drinking chocolate powder.

Serves 1

Frostbite

4–5 ice cubes
1 measure tequila
1 measure double cream
1 measure white Crème
   de Cacao
½ measure white Crème
   de Menthe
drinking chocolate
   powder, to decorate

Put the ice cubes into a cocktail shaker. Pour in the tequila, cream, Crème de Cacao, and Crème de Menthe and shake vigorously for 10 seconds. Strain into a chilled cocktail glass and sprinkle with drinking chocolate powder.

Serves 1

INDEX

Photography by
    William Reavell
Cocktails written and styled
by Wayne Collins at
19:20, 19–20 Great
Sutton Street, London
EC1V 0DR

Acknowledgements

Octopus Publishing Group Ltd./
Neil Mersh 10/ Peter
Myers/ Neil Mersh 49, 75/
William Reavell *Cover, 2,
3, 5, 6–8, 11–16, 19–21,
23, 25, 26, 28, 31, 33, 34,
37, 39, 40, 43, 45, 47, 51,
52, 55, 57–59, 61–63, 65,
67, 68, 71, 73, 76, 79, 81,
82, 84, 87, 89–91, 93, 94*